Choosing a Career in the Post Office

"Neither snow nor rain nor heat nor gloom of night stays these couriers from the swift completion of their appointed rounds."—Herodotus, ancient Greek historian. Inscribed on the General Post Office building, New York City.

Choosing a Career in the Post Office

David Chiu

The Rosen Publishing Group, Inc.
New York

*Special thanks to the United States Postal Service
for its assistance. I would also like to thank
my family and friends for their love and support.*

Published in 2001 by The Rosen Publishing Group, Inc.
29 East 21st Street, New York, NY 10010

Copyright © 2001 by The Rosen Publishing Group, Inc.

First Edition

All rights reserved. No part of this book may be reproduced in any form without permission in writing from the publisher, except by a reviewer.

Library of Congress Cataloging-in-Publication Data

Chiu, David.
   Choosing a career in the post office / David Chiu.
     p. cm.—(World of work)
   Includes bibliographical references and index.
   ISBN: 978-1-4358-8663-6
     1. Postal service—Vocational guidance—United States. 2. Postal service—United States—Employees. [1. Postal service—Vocational guidance. 2. Vocational guidance.] I. Title. II. World of work (New York, N.Y.).
   HE6499 .C33 2000
   383'.145'02373—dc21
                                                00-009459

Manufactured in the United States of America

Contents

	Introduction	6
1	The World of the Postal Service	9
2	Getting Started	21
3	As a Postal Service Employee . . .	28
4	Window Clerk	33
5	Mail Carrier	39
6	Behind-the-Scenes Jobs	44
7	Other Postal Service Jobs	49
	Glossary	57
	For More Information	60
	For Further Reading	62
	Index	63

Introduction

It is easy to take mail for granted because it has always been a part of our everyday lives. But imagine a world without mail delivery. Your birthday card to Aunt Rita would never arrive. Businesses would be affected tremendously—how would products be shipped and paid for? How would Grandma receive her monthly Social Security check from the government?

You may have an idea about how a post office operates. A window clerk sells you stamps for mail and weighs your packages. You may see postal workers loading and hauling mail from the rear of the post office. On your block, you probably see mail carriers making deliveries. However, did you know that the post office operates twenty-four hours a day, seven days a week?

The United States Postal Service is one of the country's largest employers, with a total of 797,795 career employees in 1999. Clerks and carriers make up a majority of the workforce within the Postal Service. There are, however, other important post office jobs, such as mail handlers, mail processors, and flat-sorting operators—all of whom are involved

Abraham Lincoln once worked for the U.S. Post Office.

in the sorting, processing, and distributing of mail. In addition, there are craft, professional, and managerial positions at the post office.

Former United States presidents Abraham Lincoln, William McKinley, and Harry S. Truman were once postal workers, and Benjamin Franklin was America's first postmaster. Other former postal workers include animator Walt Disney, singer Bing Crosby, author William Faulkner, and aviator Charles Lindbergh.

Do you think that you may be interested in pursuing a career that serves the public and is both personally and professionally rewarding? Entry-level jobs are open to anyone regardless of previous experience. Each year, thousands of people apply for jobs in the United States Postal Service. Why? Because the Postal Service offers good salaries, excellent benefits, and job security.

Choosing a Career in the Post Office

This book will describe some of the entry-level craft positions at the Postal Service. Craft employees are workers who are represented by a union that negotiates with the United States Postal Service (USPS) over wages and working conditions. The popular craft positions include mail carriers, clerks, and mail handlers. The book also lists the various professional and managerial occupations within the Postal Service, and it will guide you in how to pursue a job within this field. The book will also explain what happens after you are hired in America's largest and busiest government agency.

1

The World of the Postal Service

The United States Postal Service (USPS) has been in existence for over 200 years—ever since colonial times. Although it is part of the federal government, the Postal Service has operated as an independent agency since 1971.

The United States Postal Service at a Glance

There are 38,169 post offices and 331 processing plants nationwide that sort and ship mail. The Postal Service provides delivery and pickup for over 130 million households and businesses. In 1999, the USPS handled a total of 201,576 billion pieces of mail and earned a revenue of $63 billion. The Postal Service handles approximately 41 percent of the world's volume of mail.

Currently, there are about 797,795 career employees working for the Postal Service. On average, a postal worker remains with the Postal Service for fifteen years. There are approximately 292,400 clerks and 296,888 city and rural mail carriers. If the

There are 38,169 post office buildings nationwide.

Postal Service were a private business, it would be the tenth largest business in the United States.

The Role of Mail in American History

The development of mail service mirrors the growth of the United States. Before the invention of the telegraph and telephone, mail played a crucial part in communication. As the nation grew, so did ways to improve mail service. In the 1800s, methods of transportation such as the stagecoach, steamboat, and railroad increased the swiftness and dependability of mail delivery. The famed Pony Express of 1860-1861 delivered letters on horseback between the Midwest and West Coast. The invention of the automobile and the use of airplanes in the early part of the twentieth century helped distribute mail at a faster pace and over wider distances. Today, trucks and planes continue to be the biggest carriers of mail.

In the latter part of the twentieth century, in response to the increase in mail volume and the rise in manpower costs, the Post Office Department (as it was then known) took major steps to make the processing of mail more efficient. In the 1950s, the Post Office Department introduced sorting and face-canceling machines, which arrange letters in the same direction and print lines over the postage so it cannot be used again. The advent of the ZIP code in 1963, which consists of a five-digit code that identifies a specific postal region, paved the way for mail to be processed mechanically. In 1982, the first computer-driven, single-line optical

character reader (OCR) was installed to read and sort mail much faster. Today, the Postal Service continues to invest in technology—such as installing machines to read handwritten addresses—that will improve service and productivity. Stamp vending machines allow customers to purchase stamps without having to wait in line. In 1999, the Postal Service instituted PC Postage, which allows postage to be purchased and printed using personal computers and the Internet.

The trend toward automation (using machines to perform the tasks of workers) may threaten the traditional postal jobs, though machines can never replace the personalized services for which the post office has been known. People will still be needed to handle and distribute the increasingly large volume of mail and to operate special machinery.

Stamp vending machines allow people to purchase stamps without having to wait in line at the post office.

How Mail Is Delivered

To understand the specific jobs in the Postal Service, it is important to know exactly how mail is delivered.

✔ The mail carrier arrives by truck and empties the day's mail from the collection box. Then he or she returns to the nearest local post office with that mail. When the carrier arrives at the local post office, the mail is sorted and loaded onto a truck that takes the mail to the sectional center facility, a place that processes and distributes mail for post offices in a designated geographic area.

✔ When the mail arrives at the sectional center facility, mail handlers unload the sacks of mail and transport them into the post office. Inside, they place the mail onto a moving conveyor belt where the mail is culled, or separated, according to size and type (letters, oversized envelopes, and magazines). Parcels are canceled and postmarked by hand.

✔ Letters travel to a machine that cancels postage. Called the face canceler, the machine arranges the letters so they face one way and cancels the stamps by printing black, wavy lines on them so they cannot be used again. A postmark contains the name of the city where the letter has been processed, a three- or five-number ZIP code, and the time and date the letter was processed.

✔ A computerized machine called the ZIP mail translator sorts handwritten letters. The operator pushes the buttons on a keyboard to guide the letters into the appropriate bins for delivery, according to region. Machines called optical character readers (OCRs) read letters with typewritten addresses. OCRs then spray marks called a bar code on the envelopes. Then bar code sorters read the code and direct the letters to their proper destinations.

✔ These letters are then bundled for delivery onto trucks that transport the outgoing mail to the airport. The sacks of mail and packages are loaded onto the airplane bound for the destination city.

✔ When the plane arrives, the mailbags are unloaded from the plane and loaded into a mail truck that delivers the mail to that city's sectional center facility. There, the mail is again sorted and transported for delivery to the local post offices according to ZIP code.

✔ At the local post office, the mail carrier gets a load of new mail bound for his or her assigned route. He or she then arranges the mail in the order that it will be delivered, bundles the mail, and goes on his or her rounds.

Employment Outlook

Because the United States Postal Service relies on automation to process mail faster and cut down on operating costs, employment is expected to grow very slowly. In 1999, there were 797,795 career employees compared to 792,041 in 1998—an increase of only 0.7 percent. Machines are now able to perform the tasks that once were done manually by workers.

Ironically, the volume of mail is expected to rise because technology is making the processing and delivery of mail faster. Keep in mind that these technological advancements (plus the growth of Internet commerce) means that more mail will be processed. This may require additional personnel.

While the availability of some traditional entry-level sorting and clerical jobs will be limited, there will be a need for new, skilled workers who are able to handle special machinery.

Actor John Ratzenberger, who portrayed Cliff Clavin on the popular television show *Cheers*, would be classified as a full-time career bargaining worker.

How Postal Workers Are Classified

Postal workers are classified according to their work schedules:

✔ Full-time career bargaining workers. These employees work the normal forty-hour/five-days-a-week schedule. Full-time workers are career employees and are entitled to full benefits. They are represented by unions.

✔ Part-time flexible workers. These are like trainees who will eventually become full-time career employees. Flexible workers can also work full-time when another position is established. They may work less or more than forty hours depending on the type of job, and they are paid at an hourly rate.

✔ Part-time regulars. These employees work less than forty hours but have a set schedule like full-time workers. They can be elevated to full-time status.

✔ Casual workers. Casual workers are hired to fill a temporary need during busy times of the year such as the Christmas season or when full-time employees go on vacation. They do not have to take the Postal Service exam. As a casual worker, you may work for a couple of weeks. If you want to become a full-time career worker, you must take the Postal Service exam.

Unions

As a career postal employee, your salary is determined by agreements between the Postal Service and the unions that represent the craft employees. There are four major unions: the American Postal Workers Union, the National Association of Letter Carriers, the National Postal Handlers Union, and the National Rural Carriers Association. These unions negotiate with the Postal Service on behalf of their members on issues such as wages, working conditions, and health and pension benefits.

Salaries and Benefits

A career in the postal industry is attractive to many people because of the excellent salary and benefits package the Postal Service offers. These benefits include:

✔ A competitive salary with continuous increases. In the last few years, the salary for employees in entry-level positions has ranged from approximately $24,000 to $26,000.

✔ Vacation time. In your first year as a postal employee, you are entitled to thirteen vacation days a year. After three years of employment, you are entitled to twenty days off a year; after fifteen years of service, you receive twenty-six vacation days annually.

✔ Sick days. An employee can have thirteen sick days per year.

✔ Holidays. Career postal workers get ten paid holidays annually.

✔ Life insurance. Postal employees receive free life insurance.

✔ Health benefits. The Postal Service pays for most of the employee's health costs.

✔ Retirement program. When you are hired, you will be covered under the Federal Employees Retirement System (FERS), which includes Social Security benefits, a tax-favored savings plan, disability benefits, and a generous pension.

Canada's Postal System

Canada's postal system, called the Canada Post Corporation, was a part of the Canadian government until it was incorporated by Parliament in 1981. It is the country's fourth leading employer, with approximately 63,000 employees. Canada Post handled 9.6 billion pieces of mail between 1998 and 1999. Like its American equivalent, Canada Post is moving in the direction of making mail processing and delivery more efficient.

Canada Post offers a wide variety of employment opportunities, including jobs in mailing operations, marketing and sales, finance, information systems, human resources, communications, and administration. Canada Post offers excellent salaries, benefits, and growth opportunities. To encourage good job performance, Canada Post created the Learning Institute in 1994. This institute helps employees develop and improve their job skills, and offers a range of new learning and developmental opportunities.

To learn more about employment opportunities at Canada Post, contact your local postal station or visit their Web site: *http://www.canadapost.ca*.

Among other requirements, you must be eighteen years or older to be employed by the U.S. Postal Service.

2

Getting Started

In order to become eligible for employment in the United States Postal Service, you must meet the following job requirements:

✔ You must be eighteen years or older by the time you are hired.

✔ You must be a United States citizen or a permanent resident alien (documentation is required).

✔ You will be asked to take a physical examination if the job requires physical work.

✔ You must pass a drug test.

✔ You must have a current driver's license if the work involves driving a vehicle.

✔ There is no educational requirement for an entry-level position. If you are seeking a professional position, a college degree is required.

✔ Your background will be checked for any criminal history.

✔ A safe driving record is required if you are driving at work.

How Do You Find a Post Office Job?

Since the Postal Service offers attractive salaries and benefits, getting a job at the post office is difficult. Thousands of people apply for jobs, but only a small percentage are hired. The Postal Service will first look within its current pool of employees to fill vacant positions.

The Postal Service Exam

If the local post office needs to fill entry-level positions, it will make an announcement to the public and will schedule an exam called the 470 battery test, which covers positions such as clerk, carrier, and handler. In order to apply for a job, you must take the exam first, no matter how qualified you are. The exam is scheduled infrequently, depending on local hiring needs. You might have to wait two or three years until the next exam.

Check often with your local post office to find out if there are any available positions and when the next exam date will be. Announcements of openings and the exam are posted on post office lobby bulletin boards.

Other Sources of Information

Some post offices have a human resources or employment placement division. You could also write to the district office of the Postal Service in your city,

Entry-level postal employees are required to take an exam called the 470 battery test.

or check your local federal job information center or state employment office for further information. Job announcements are also publicized in newspapers, through community organizations, and on the Postal Service Web site: *http://www.usps.com* (for professional and managerial positions only).

Try speaking to a Postal Service employee such as your mail carrier. Since they already work for the Postal Service, employees can give you information and advice on how they found their jobs and how to get your foot in the door.

Applying for a Job

When an examination is scheduled, apply as soon as possible since there is a deadline for the application process.

Filling Out Form 2479

You need to go to the post office or postal district that is offering the exam and pick up the PS 2479 application form. On one part of the form, you fill out your name, address, birth date, phone number, title of examination, and which post office you are applying for (if you are unsure how to fill out this form, have a Postal Service employee help you). On the admission card part of the form, you fill out your Social Security number in addition to the same information that you put on the application card.

Do not separate the form or the post office will not accept it. Return the entire form to your post office as soon as possible because the filing deadline for the application may be coming up in only a few days. The post office will mail your admission card back to you with the date and time of the test, where the test will be given, instructions, and sample questions. For further practice, there are test preparation books that you can find at libraries and bookstores. These books contain sample test questions similar to the ones on the actual exam. They offer techniques on how to memorize addresses and follow oral instructions.

The Exam

On the days before the exam date, make sure you know where the testing center is so that you will not get lost and waste valuable time. If you are unsure, call the testing center for directions. Make sure that you get a good night's sleep prior to the exam. And remember to arrive at the testing center early so that you can stay focused and relaxed. Wear comfortable

Getting Started

clothes. Bring your admission card, two number 2 pencils with erasers, and a photo ID.

The 470 Battery Test

The 470 battery test is the standard examination for the entry-level postal positions of window clerk, mail carrier, machine distribution clerk, mail processor, flat-sorting machine operator, and mark-up clerk. It measures your reading comprehension, memorization skills, and your ability to follow instructions. As you begin the exam, pay careful attention to the test examiner. Answer the questions correctly and as quickly as possible.

The 470 battery test measures your ability to distinguish and memorize addresses, and to follow oral instructions. It consists of four parts. Part A involves address checking, in which you must distinguish between addresses that may be similar (for example, you might have to note the difference between 2741 Greenwich Avenue and 2471 Greenwich Avenue). Part B requires you to memorize addresses, which is key in sorting and delivering mail. In part C, you will be tested on your ability to operate sorting machines. Part D will test your ability to listen and follow spoken instructions that are similar to what you will hear from a supervisor.

Your exam is scored electronically. Applicants are notified of their results approximately eight weeks after the exam. If you pass, your name will be placed on a register, a list of names ranked from the highest score to the lowest. A score of 70 is passing; however, the competition is so tough that only a higher score of 90 to 100 points will elevate

Brush up on your interview skills by practicing with a family member or friend.

you above the rest. (Also consider this: Military veterans who take the exam are automatically given free additional points on the test.) Your name will be on the register for approximately two years (if nothing happens during that time, you can reapply). If there is a job opening and your name is at the top of the register, you will be screened and scheduled for an interview.

The Screening and Interviewing Process

The Postal Service will screen you to see if you are a suitable candidate to work there. You will fill out an employee application form that will be reviewed as part of a background check that will include your work history. You will also be tested for drugs and take a medical exam.

Next, you will be interviewed. The interview helps the Postal Service determine if you are the best candidate for the position. This is your opportunity to tell the Postal Service why you should be hired. You should try to prepare for the interview beforehand. There are books that can help you brush up on your interview skills. Get a family member or a friend to help you practice. Be confident—all you have to prove to the interviewer is that you are a dedicated, serious, and hard working person for the job.

The interviewer will probably ask you questions about your background, previous work history, your personal goals, and why you are applying for a postal job. The interview will also give you a chance to make a case for why you should be hired and to ask the interviewer questions about the nature and specifics of the job and whether there are advancement opportunities. At the completion of the interview, find out when you will be notified of a decision to hire you if the interviewer has not already mentioned it. Thank the person for his or her time and consideration. If you meet the criteria, a job offer will be made to you.

As a Postal Service Employee . . .

According to the Postal Service, its employees are major contributors to the success of the organization. That is why the Postal Service places great emphasis on developing a knowledgeable and skilled workforce through its training and development programs. New employees serve a ninety-day initial trial period of employment during which their supervisors and fellow colleagues train them. These new hires learn about procedures and regulations and how to become efficient at their jobs. They also learn about growth opportunities within the Postal Service.

Training and Development

There are three categories that fall under training and development:

> ✔ Job training. The purpose of job training is to improve the employee's performance. Examples of job training include postal orientation, which familiarizes the trainee

with the policies and procedures of the Postal Service. Job training is very important; refusal to participate or less than satisfactory performance during the training period can affect an employee's chances for advancement.

✔ Self-development. Self-development enables the employee to gain career skills that are not directly related to his or her current job. For example, a letter carrier might take a foreign language course so that he or she can communicate better with customers not fluent in English; a secretary can participate in a seminar on leadership; a mail processor can take a CD-ROM course in computer software.

✔ Job experience. Job experience can contribute to maintaining and improving an employee's knowledge, skills, and abilities. This may entail additional and special assignments and projects.

Training Facilities

The Postal Service provides training facilities that are like academies for newly hired employees. These centers train and prepare workers for the real world of working within the Postal Service. The following is a description of the major training centers in the United States.

✔ Postal employee development centers (PEDCs). There are over 200 PEDCs that make up a huge bulk of the Postal Service training across the country. The goal of the PEDCs is to foster good employee job performance. They offer a wide variety of courses and programs that provide essential training and career counseling for new hires.

✔ National Center for Employee Development (NCED). Located in Norman, Oklahoma, this center oversees programs and offers courses in the areas of technical maintenance, processing, and technology.

✔ William Bolger Center for Leadership Development. This facility trains managers and supervisors in dealing with fellow colleagues and coping with other issues in the area of leadership and management. Postal inspectors are also trained at this facility.

✔ Postal Satellite Training Network. This system network transmits training programs such as lectures and demonstrations by satellite. This enables many employees to receive training at one time via television.

Promotions and Transfers

When you have worked at the Postal Service for a year, you become eligible to apply for other positions. When new jobs are announced, postal employees are given first preference. As with any job, if you want to be promoted, you must have a good work record. Poor job performance will affect your chances of advancement. You must prove that you are able to follow your supervisor's instructions, strive for excellence, and demonstrate leadership

The U.S. Postal Service trains and prepares new workers at their PEDCs (postal employees development centers).

abilities. Maintaining good relationships with the people you work with is crucial. Take the time to learn new things along with your current job.

To be considered for a promotion, you fill out a form called the PS 991 when there is a job opening. You indicate on the form your experience, previous work history, and why you are the best candidate for the position. Your application will be subject to review.

As a postal employee who gains experience over time, you are eligible for a transfer to another post office or a reassignment to a position that suits your skills. A transfer might be the result of a desire to move to another area or for personal and family reasons. You can move to another post office in your area or anywhere else in the country. If you want to transfer or be reassigned, you must apply in writing and state your reasons for transfer, which will then be evaluated. If you do not succeed in getting a transfer the first time, you can always reapply later.

As you have read, the career opportunities within the post office are numerous and diverse. Whether you are interested in becoming a mail carrier, flat-sorting operator, or a computer specialist, you will be part of a very large team dedicated to delivering mail better and faster. The new century and the continuous growth of technology will create new challenges and opportunities within the Postal Service.

Be aware—the competition is rough for entry-level jobs. So many people are applying for a limited number of available positions. If you really want to work in the post office, start thinking and planning now. Visit a post office and seek information. Remember, the job will not come to you—you have to go to it.

If you are interested in working in the post office, you will be making good money and have job security so long as you do your job well. Most important, you will be part of something very important that helps bring people together—the mail.

4

Window Clerk

I have been a postal employee for over ten years now. The thing I love most about my job is helping customers. We offer many different services at the post office, so for the average customer, mail delivery and policies can be confusing. My job is to make the mailing experience pleasant for customers.

People assume that the window clerk is someone who just sells stamps and weighs packages. While those duties do make up a huge part of the job, there are other duties I sometimes perform—such as sorting and distributing mail—that are out of the public view. With so much variety, the job rarely becomes boring.

I sometimes get my share of complaints from customers about the service. You have to get used to it. Being a window clerk requires you to be patient and respectful. I used to work in retail before working here. But for me, being

A window clerk's primary duties are to sell stamps and other postal products, and to determine the right postage amounts for letters and packages.

and staying friendly is so easy in this job. I enjoy talking to people of different ages and backgrounds. This is the best job I've ever had. What more can I ask for than a job that lets me interact with people and provides a good living?
—Yvonne Smith, window clerk, New York, NY

A Window Clerk's Duties and Responsibilities

Your main function as a window clerk is to sell stamps and to determine the proper postage for letters and packages. You also check to see if a parcel is suitable for mailing—if it is packaged properly to prevent damage during the handling and processing. You answer customers' questions about delivery service and restrictions. You are responsible for keeping track of the amount of postage stamps that are sold. In addition, you provide mail-related services such as insuring, certifying, and registering mail, as well as Express Mail and Priority Mail. The clerk also sells other postal products such as postal cards, aerogrammes, stamped envelopes, mailing boxes, and money orders. Window clerks also handle the rental of post office boxes and collect the rental fees.

As a window clerk, you may have other responsibilities that are out of the public view. You might check and adjust the settings on postage meters and assist in census matters. You may function as the distribution clerk who sorts and distributes incoming and outgoing mail. The

A window clerk may have other responsibilities that are not in the public view.

window clerk may have to transport mail from one part of the building to another using a hand truck. If necessary, you might be called on to substitute as a mail carrier in emergency situations.

Working Conditions

Some window clerks say that dealing with the public is the most rewarding aspect of this position. The window clerk is the Postal Service's connection to the public. In a high-profile position such as this, you have to be a people person. Courtesy, friendliness, and respect must be maintained even when dealing with angry, rude customers. The ability to work under pressure is important when the hours and the lines are long, especially at large post offices located in business districts and during Christmas and holiday weekends. Though there is little physical activity, you will spend most of the day standing and may on occasion have to perform other types of work that are physical.

There are many advantages to this job. Because of the variety of duties, boredom is kept to a minimum. You work in a clean, well-ventilated and well-lit space as opposed to working with noisy machinery in the background. Most clerks rarely work at night.

Currently, the starting salary for a window clerk is approximately $26,000 a year. Over a period of time, a window clerk can advance to a position as supervisor.

A mail carrier is responsible for delivering and collecting mail.

5

Mail Carrier

I remember when I was a child, we had a letter carrier named Lynn who delivered the mail on our block. At the time, it was very rare to see a female letter carrier. She was in her fifties and had worked for the Postal Service for twenty years. Lynn always made her rounds on time, even when the weather was unpleasant. She knew everyone in the neighborhood and she addressed each person by his or her first name. Whenever Lynn saw me, she would greet me with a smile. She even took the time to talk to people who had questions about mail service. Her dedication to the job and her kindness were qualities I never forgot.

Years later, after I graduated college, I worked in public relations for two years, but I knew in my heart that I wanted to work at the post office and become a mail carrier like Lynn. I liked the idea of being out-of-doors and interacting with people. When a postal exam was announced in my area, I filed an application and took the test. After scoring high, I went in for an interview and was later hired.

After some on-the-job training and after working as a part-time substitute, I finally became a full-time worker and got my own route to cover when one of the veteran carriers retired. As I became familiar with the job, knowing people's names and addresses seemed as normal as knowing my own birthday. At 6 AM I go to the post office to sort and bundle mail. Then I deliver the mail on foot. My number one priority is making my deliveries and collections on time. After finishing my rounds, I go to the collection boxes, gather up all the day's mail, and bring it back to the post office to be handled later at central processing.

I love seeing people's faces light up when I deliver the mail to them. It just shows that the mail still holds an important place in people's everyday lives.
—Wendy Randall, mail carrier, Seattle, WA

A Mail Carrier's Duties and Responsibilities

A mail carrier is responsible for delivering and collecting mail in a prompt manner. Dressed in a blue

Many mail carriers make their rounds by truck, others by foot; some use both.

and grey uniform emblazoned with the Postal Service logo, the carrier is probably the most recognizable person on your street next to a police officer.

As a mail carrier, your day begins at the post office early in the morning. You receive a bundle of mail and arrange it by address in the proper sequential order along your delivery route.

You then make rounds either by foot or by car or both (if you must drive, you need a valid driver's license and must have a good driving record). In residential areas, the mail carrier will make one delivery a day. In a business district, delivery sometimes occurs twice a day. You make your deliveries to people's homes, to curbside and roadside boxes, or in the lobbies of office buildings. Along the way, you pick up another load of mail, which has been stored in a relay box and needs to be delivered.

Choosing a Career in the Post Office

A mail carrier collects monies for postage—regular mail and collect on delivery mail (C.O.D). If a customer is not present to receive a package or sign for certified mail, you need to leave a note for the recipient indicating that a delivery attempt was made. A mail carrier picks up mail left in residential and business mailboxes and collection boxes. Then you return to the post office with the collected mail and monies and receipts of the day. At the post office, you separate the letters and parcels to be sorted and processed later at the central processing center. You might also have to do other administrative tasks at the post office.

A rural mail carrier's duties are very similar to a city carrier's, though most rural carriers drive their routes. The rural carrier delivers to roadside mailboxes and picks up outgoing mail. Some rural carriers function as mobile post offices—they sell stamps, accept packages, and insure, certify, and register mail.

Working Conditions

As a mail carrier, you start work early in the morning but finish by the afternoon—once the deliveries and administrative tasks are done at the post office. Being outside is enjoyable, though at times you may encounter hazardous conditions, depending on where you live. The most frequent danger for a mail carrier is getting bitten by a dog. Working outdoors, you will be under little supervision, unlike working inside the post office. But there is also no manager or supervisor you can turn to if there is trouble.

Like working as a window clerk, being a carrier is a high-profile position within the Postal Service. You must maintain a friendly and respectful attitude toward the people you encounter on your route. You are responsible for answering customers' questions about delivery service and providing people with forms (like a change of address card) upon request. As a mail carrier, you are the link between the community and the post office. Some carriers participate in community programs like neighborhood watch programs. Currently, the starting salary for a city or rural mail carrier is about $26,000 a year. He or she can later be promoted to a supervisory position.

6

Behind-the-Scenes Jobs

There are many different postal positions that take place behind-the-scenes. Some of these occupations include machine operators and mail processors.

Mail Handler

Mail handlers help move mail by loading and unloading sacks of incoming and outgoing mail that are transported via trucks or train. Mail handlers separate mail according to size and type: letters, parcels, magazines, books. They place mail on conveyor belts, which send the mail to be processed.

This job requires a fair amount of heavy lifting; some mail may weigh as much as seventy pounds. Applicants are required to take a physical exam. Mail handlers often work at nights or on weekends. New mail handlers earn about $24,600 a year and often seek future careers as clerks or mail carriers.

Machine Distribution Clerk

If you are hired as a machine distribution clerk, your main duty is to operate a letter-sorting machine. On

A machine distribution clerk operates the letter-sorting machine.

a keyboard attached to the machine, you press the appropriate keys to send the mail to the appropriate mail bin. You read the addresses on the envelopes from right to left at a rate of fifty letters per minute. Careful attention must be paid because you are determining which route each letter is intended for.

Being a machine distribution clerk also involves loading, unloading, and moving mail. You might also have to operate face-canceling machines and maintain mailing records of items that require special services such as registered and certified mail. On some occasions, you may need to substitute for a window clerk and deal with customers.

If you are interested in becoming a machine distribution clerk, you must have good vision and be able to type. Good hand-eye coordination is important. You are surrounded by noisy machines that are continuously in operation. The entry-level salary for a distribution clerk is approximately $26,000 a year. As the Postal Service continues to adopt new forms of technology in the processing of mail, there is a chance for growth with this job.

Mail Processor

As a mail processor, your main duty will be operating automated equipment such as optical character readers and bar code sorters that automatically recognize and sort mail. You will be responsible for fixing and clearing jams in machines, sweeping mail from the bins, and placing and bundling mail that will eventually be loaded onto transport units.

Mail processing is not a very strenuous job, though depending on the task required, you may find yourself doing a lot of standing and lifting. Mail processors usually work nights, when most mail is processed. A beginning mail processor can make about $24,600 a year and can advance to the position of clerk, mail handler, or supervisor over time.

Flat-Sorting Machine Operator

The job of a flat-sorting machine operator involves controlling a machine with a special keyboard that sorts and distributes flats (large mail such as

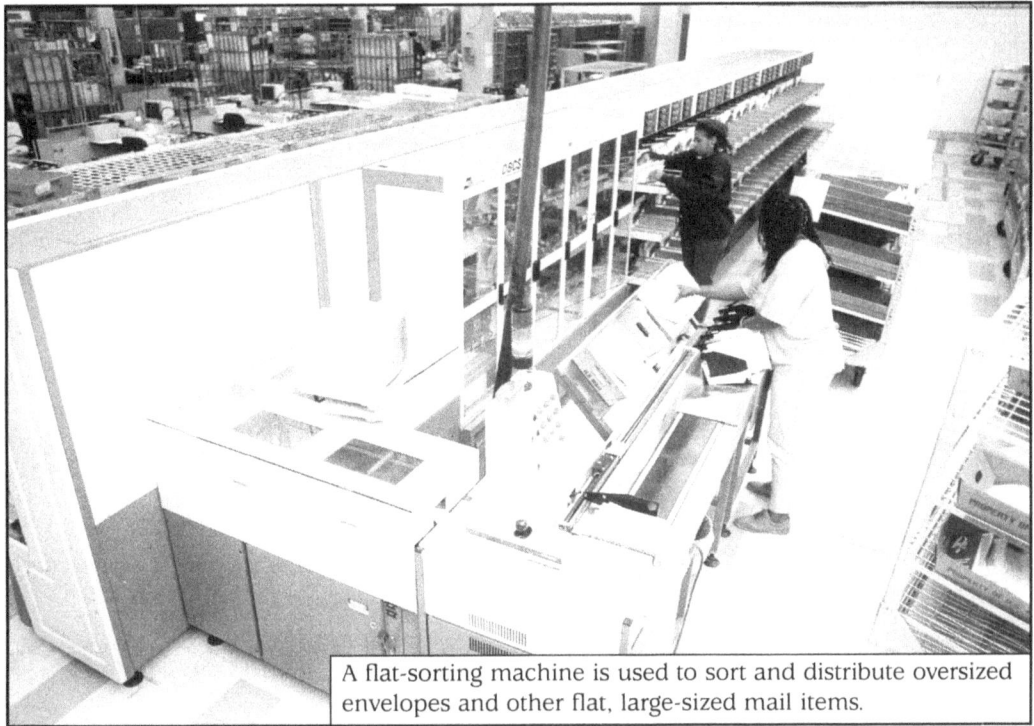

A flat-sorting machine is used to sort and distribute oversized envelopes and other flat, large-sized mail items.

oversized envelopes). Flats are fed into machines and then the operator directs the flats to their proper destinations according to ZIP codes. The flat-sorting machine operator might also bundle, load, and unload mail. You also may work on other machines that function as sorters.

Accuracy and attention to detail are needed for this job. Good vision is also very important. The job may entail some physical work, but it is not too strenuous. Operators may work nights or weekends. The starting salary for a flat-sorting machine operator is about $26,000 a year. As you gain experience, you can be promoted to a position of supervisor.

Mark-Up Clerk

Ever wonder how the Postal Service is able to deliver mail even if the addressee has moved away?

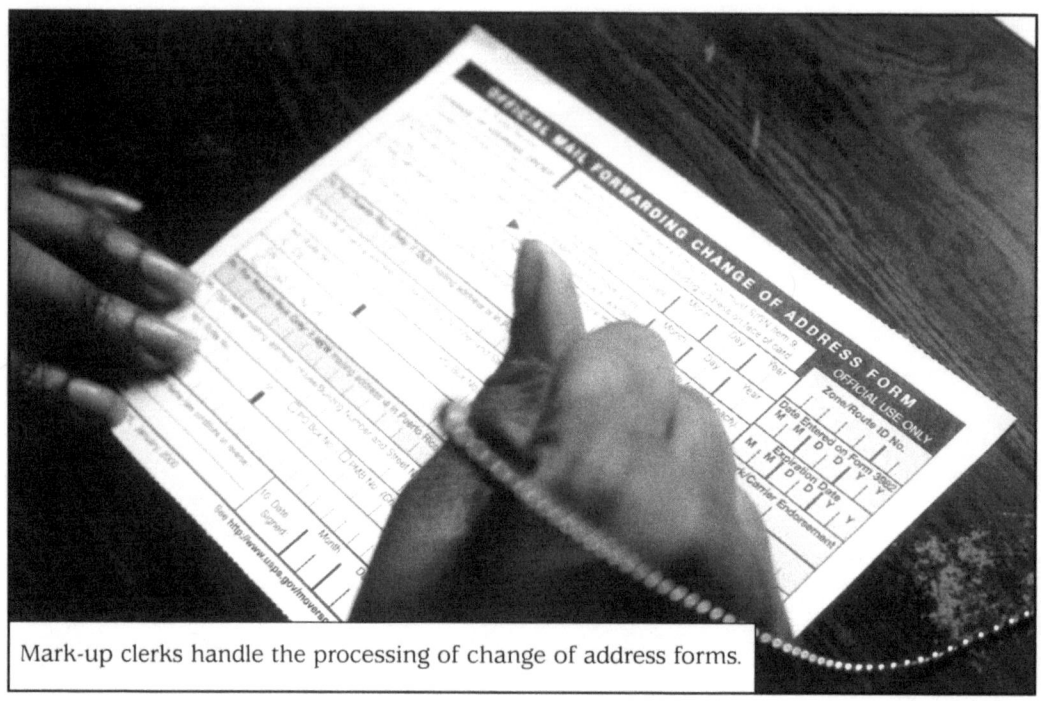
Mark-up clerks handle the processing of change of address forms.

That is the job of a mark-up clerk. Mark-up clerks input the information from the change of address form that has been filled out by the person who is moving. This information is stored in a computer. They also prepare forms for address correction and process mail that is undeliverable because of incorrect or inaccurate information. Mark-up clerks stick labels with the newly corrected address onto previously undeliverable mail.

To become a mark-up clerk, you need strong data entry and typing skills. Knowledge of computers and the ability to work with machines is also important. Like a distribution clerk, you need to be able to work efficiently and accurately since there is a lot of mail to process. The salary of a starting mark-up clerk is approximately $24,600 a year. Eventually, a hardworking mark-up clerk can be promoted to distribution clerk, flat-sorting machine operator, or supervisor.

7

Other Postal Service Jobs

In addition to the popular entry-level craft positions described earlier in the book, there is a diverse range of other occupations within the Postal Service. They include other craft positions such as motor vehicle operator and automotive mechanic. Professional and managerial positions such as electronic engineer or postmaster require a college degree, previous experience in the field, or both.

Craft Positions

You have already read about some of the craft positions, such as mail carrier, mail handler, and markup clerk. Craft employees are those represented by unions that negotiate with the Postal Service over wages and working conditions. Some craft positions are in the job category of technical maintenance. For example, an automotive mechanic makes sure that vehicles like trucks are functioning properly so mail can be transported.

The job of an electronics technician is to troubleshoot mechanical and circuitry problems. Like the other entry-level jobs previously described, vacant craft jobs and the accompanying exams are announced at the post office or in the newspapers, and follow the same application procedures.

Here is a brief list of some other craft jobs:

- ✔ Blacksmith
- ✔ Carpenter
- ✔ Custodian
- ✔ Electrician
- ✔ Engine mechanic
- ✔ Firefighter
- ✔ Maintenance worker
- ✔ Mason
- ✔ Motor vehicle operator
- ✔ Painter
- ✔ Plumber
- ✔ Security guard

Professional Positions

These specialized occupations require professional degrees and experience. They are jobs that are open to Postal Service employees (who are given first preference) and to the public in the event that the jobs cannot be filled internally. Openings are announced at the post office, in classified advertisements, and on the USPS Web site. Seekers of professional positions should fill out the PS Form 2591 and submit a résumé. Below is a partial list of the professional positions available at the Postal Service.

Architect Engineer
The successful candidate should have experience in architecture, engineering, and building construction. (Salary range: $53,900 to $73,500.)

Computer Systems Specialist
This job provides a great opportunity to work with technology that is available only in companies of this size. The computer systems specialist should possess strong software systems programming abilities and technical support experience. (Salary based on previous experience.)

Economist
This person oversees, develops, and coordinates Postal Service economic policies, plans, projects, and goals. The economist conducts economic research relating to revenue and cost measurements. The applicant should have knowledge in the fields of economics, statistics, and quantitative and qualitative research. (Salary range: $59,400 to $81,000.)

Electronic Commerce Specialist
This person deals with business on the Internet as it relates to the Postal Service by developing programs, projects, and strategies. The specialist should have the ability to review customer inquiries, do research, and provide feedback. (Salary range: $53,900 to $73,500.)

Postal inspectors investigate criminal offenses such as mail fraud and the sending of illegal materials.

Electronic Engineer

Successful candidates must demonstrate knowledge of electrical and electromechanical systems that can be used on mail processing equipment. The engineer should be able to design circuitry and write software programs. (Salary range: $53,900 to $73,500.)

Marketing Specialist

This position involves planning, developing, and carrying out marketing plans to enhance customer acceptance and to increase revenue. (Salary range: $59,400 to $81,000.)

Mechanical Engineer

The applicant should know about mechanical engineering principles, procedures, and practices. (Salary range: $59,400 to $81,000.)

Postal Inspector

Postal inspectors investigate and prevent criminal offenses in the processing and delivery of mail, including fraud and illegal mailings. They are the Postal Service's version of law enforcement. Postal inspectors also check on the financial costs of postal operations and develop programs to ensure work efficiency. A degree in law or accounting is required for a postal inspector job. An applicant for a postal inspector position should be in good physical health, have good vision, and should have no criminal record. A driver's license is required. (Salary range: $42,700 to $60,600.)

Psychologist

The candidate for this position should have experience in applied industrial/organizational psychology and in various approaches to evaluating employee performance. A graduate degree in industrial/organizational psychology (or related area of study) is required. (Salary range: $48,300 to $65,700.)

Security Engineering Technician

The person should possess knowledge of audio/video transmission and recording equipment. He or she will work on basic electronic test equipment. (Salary range: $38,200 to $50,500.)

Speechwriter

This person assists in the research, writing, and editing of speeches and other editorial materials for the officers of the Postal Service. The candidate should have the ability to write and edit communications for publications, speeches, and printed and video materials regarding postal policies and programs. (Salary range: $53,900 to $73,500.)

Women's Program Specialist

Applicants for this position should be familiar with equal employment opportunity laws, policies, and procedures. This specialist should be able to monitor, interpret, and analyze affirmative action laws and regulations, and should have the ability to develop plans and policies. (Salary range: $53,900 to $73,500.)

Managerial Positions

Applicants interested in managerial positions must demonstrate the ability to work with other people and to lead. Candidates should have the skills and experience required for the jobs. These positions are usually filled internally—at various post offices nationwide or at the USPS headquarters in Washington, DC. Candidates should fill out a PS Form 991 to apply for these jobs. The following is a list of some of the managerial jobs mentioned on the USPS's Web site.

Accounting Operations Manager

This person manages districtwide planning and operation of accounting programs, policies, procedures, and processes. The applicant should have knowledge of policies and procedures related to postal accounting, including timekeeping and payroll, and of postal computerized financial systems. (Salary range: $48,300 to $65,700.)

Customer Services Manager

This person manages the activities of a medium-size carrier station or branch. Provides delivery and collection services within, or sometimes beyond, a normal geographic area. He or she manages window and box services, mail distribution and dispatch, and the processing or sale of nonpostal products. (Salary range: $43,700 to $59,400.)

Distribution Operations Manager

This person manages all automated, mechanized, and/or manual mail processing and distribution operations at a very large size mail processing center/facility. Interested persons must know about mail processing and distribution operations, and mail policies and procedures. (Salary range: $51,100 to $69,700.)

Human Resources Manager

This person manages district human resources, coordinates activities related to labor relations and equal opportunity employment. The candidate should have knowledge of human resources policies, procedures, and programs, including recruitment and employment training. (Salary range: $56,600 to $77,100.)

Maintenance Operations Manager

This person manages all maintenance operations. He or she must have knowledge of current building and equipment maintenance methods and practices. (Salary range: $51,100 to $69,700.)

Postmaster

A postmaster is the general manager of his or her post office. The postmaster is responsible for making sure that postal operations run smoothly. He or she delegates duties to subordinates, hires new employees, makes up work schedules, and evaluates work performances. The postmaster enforces post office rules and regulations, and fields customer queries and complaints. (Salary range: $41,700 to $56,700.)

Glossary

aerogramme Lightweight sheet that is folded and used to send a message overseas.

airmail The movement of mail via aircraft.

bar code sorter Machine that reads the marks sprayed by the optical character reader, then electronically directs the mail according to region.

certified mail Letter or package, the delivery of which is recorded and certified by the Postal Service for extra protection; it is designed to insure the delivery to the addressee and is cheaper than registered mail.

collect on delivery (C.O.D.) Service for mailers who need to mail an article for which they have not received payment. The amount due the sender is collected from the addressee, and the Postal Service returns the amount due to the sender.

cull To remove nonletter mail (parcels, odd-shaped material) from letter mail by hand or machine.

Express Mail Special domestic mail service that guarantees delivery the next day.

face canceler Mail processing equipment that automatically faces letter-size mail in one direction and cancels the postage.

flat-sorting machine operator Operates a machine that sorts flats (large mail such as oversized envelopes).

Choosing a Career in the Post Office

470 battery test Examination given for entry-level positions at the Postal Service such as mail carrier and window clerk.

insured mail Service that provides coverage for lost, stolen, or damaged mail.

machine distribution clerk This person sorts and distributes mail to its proper destination with the use of machines.

mail carrier Postal employee who collects and delivers the mail in an assigned area.

mail handler Employee who loads and unloads sacks of mail to be processed, separates the mail by hand, and cancels postage.

mail processor Operates the machines that process mail.

mark-up clerk Processes undeliverable mail that has incorrect address information.

money order Similar to bank checks; a safe way to send money via the mail system.

optical character reader (OCR) Mail sorting machine that reads address information on a letter and sprays the corresponding ZIP code information onto the letter as a barcode.

oversized mail Mail that exceeds the dimensions of a letter but does not reach the dimensions of larger mail such as parcels.

parcel Mail larger than a letter in dimension that is usually enclosed in a box.

postage Amount paid for anything sent by mail.

postage due mail Mail on which additional postage is collectable on final delivery.

postal card Card with printed postage on it that can be used to send a message.

postmark Printed on the envelope, it indicates the name of the city where the letter has been processed and three numbers of the ZIP code, when it was processed (AM or PM), and the date.

postmaster Person in charge of a post office.

post office The basic organizational unit of the Postal Service that collects and delivers mail and provides retail services in a specific geographic area.

Priority Mail Special type of mail service that delivers mail in two to three days to anywhere in the United States.

register List of names of persons who have taken the 470 battery test, ranked from the highest to lowest scores; it helps the post office in the hiring process.

registered mail Service in which the sender receives a receipt at the time of the mailing, and a record is kept at the post office of address.

sectional center facility Postal facility that serves as the processing and distribution center for post offices in a specified geographic area.

window clerk Postal worker who sells stamps and determines postage behind the window of a post office; informs customers of services and restrictions.

ZIP (Zone Improvement Plan) code A system of five-digit codes that identifies the post office or metropolitan area delivery station associated with an address.

ZIP mail translator Machine that translates the operator's keystrokes into instructions that enable the machine to send the letter into the correct bin.

For More Information

In the United States

American Postal Workers Union
1300 L Street NW
Washington, DC 20005
(202) 842-4200
Web site: http://www.apwu.org

National Association of Letter Carriers
100 Indiana Avenue NW
Washington, DC 20001
(202) 393-4695
Web site: http://www.nalc.org

National Postal Mail Handlers Union
1101 Connecticut Avenue NW, Suite 500
Washington, DC 20036
(202) 833-9095
Web site: http://www.npmhu.org

National Rural Letter Carriers' Association
1630 Duke Street, Fourth Floor
Alexandria, VA 22314
(703) 684-5545
Web site: http://www.nrlca.org

United States Postal Service
475 L'Enfant Plaza SW
Washington, DC 20260
(800) JOB-USPS (for national job openings)
(800) 276-5627 (for local employment)
Web site: http://www.usps.com

In Canada

Canada Post
2701 Riverside Drive, Suite N0722
Ottawa, ON K1A 0B1
(613) 734-7575
Web site: http://www.canadapost.ca

Web Sites

Federal Jobs digest
http://www.jobsfed.com

United States Office of Personnel Management
http://www.usajobs.opm.gov

For Further Reading

Barkus, Philip. *How to Prepare for the Comprehensive Postal Exam.* Hauppauge, NY: Barron's, 1995.

Bautista, Veltisezar B. *The Book of U.S. Postal Exams.* Farmington Hills, MI: Bookhaus Publishers, 1999.

Damp, Dennis V. *Post Office Jobs: How to Get Jobs with the U.S. Postal Service.* Moon Township, PA: Bookhaven Press, 1996.

Gish, Jim (ed.). *Postal Worker Exam.* Norwalk, CT: Learning Express, 1997.

Turlington, Shannon. *Teach Yourself to Pass the Postal Service Exams in 24 Hours.* Indianapolis, IN: IDG Books Worldwide, 1999.

United States Postal Service. *Employee and Labor Relations Manual.* Washington, DC: United States Postal Service, 1999.

———. *Glossary of Postal Terms: Publication 32.* Washington, DC: United States Postal Service, 1999.

———. *History of the United States Postal Service 1775-1993.* Washington, DC: Washington, DC: United States Postal Service, 1993.

Index

B
bar code, 14

C
Canada Post Corporation, 19
culling, 14

E
exam for USPS, 17, 22, 24-25, 50
    470 battery test, 22, 25-26
    test prep books, 24

F
forms for USPS
    Form 991, 31
    Form 2479, 24
    Form 2591, 51

J
job hunting at USPS, 22-26, 27
jobs at USPS
    career employees, 6, 17
    casual workers, 17
    craft employees, 7, 8, 49-50

flat-sorting operators, 6, 25, 32, 46-47, 48
flexible workers, 17
machine distribution clerk, 25, 44-46, 48
mail carriers, 6, 8, 9, 22, 23, 25, 32, 36, 39-43, 49
mail handlers, 6, 8, 13, 22, 44, 46, 49
mail processors, 6, 25, 46
managerial positions, 7, 8, 49, 54-56
mark-up clerk, 25, 47-48, 49
part-time workers, 17
postal inspector, 30, 53
postmaster, 7, 49, 56
professional positions, 7, 8, 49, 50-54
supervisors, 37, 42, 46-47, 48
technical maintenance, 30, 49
window clerk, 6, 9, 22, 25, 33-37, 46

Choosing a Career in the Post Office

L
Learning Institute, 19

M
machines at USPS (technology)
    bar code sorters, 14
    face-canceling, 11, 14, 45
    optical character readers
        (OCRs), 12, 14, 46
    sorting machines, 11, 44
    ZIP mail translator, 14
mail, how it is delivered, 13–15
mail service, history of, 11–12

N
National Association of Letter
    Carriers, 18
National Center for Employee
    Development (NCED), 30
National Postal Handlers
    Union, 18
National Rural Carriers
    Association, 18

night work at USPS, 37, 46, 47

P
postal employee development
    centers (PEDCs), 29–30
Postal Satellite Training
    Network, 30
postmark, 14
post offices, 2, 10, 13–15
promotions and transfers at
    USPS, 30–32

S
salary and benefits at USPS, 7,
    17, 18–19
sectional center facility, 13

U
unions at USPS, 8, 17–18, 49

Z
ZIP codes, 11, 14, 15, 47

Special Thanks
Thanks to the United States Postal Service for the images it provided.

About the Author
David Chiu is a freelance writer. He lives in New York City.

Photo Credits
Cover by Thaddeus Harden. Pp. 2, 13, 20, 23, 26, 36, 38, 48 by Bob Van Lindt; p. 7 © FPG International; p. 10 by Bob Van Lindt (New York, NY), © Dennis Cody/FPG International (Ochopee, FL), © Peter Gridley/FPG International (Upperville, VA), and Richard H. Johnston/FPG International (French Glen, OR); pp. 12, 34, 41, 45, 47, 52 © U.S. Postal Service; p. 16 © Archive Photos; p. 31 © Ron Chapple/FPG International.

Layout
Geri Giordano

www.ingramcontent.com/pod-product-compliance
Lightning Source LLC
Chambersburg PA
CBHW041114070526
44584CB00002B/168